SALAMANDER

Clare Hibbert

FRANKLIN WATTS
LONDON•SYDNEY

First published in 2007 by Franklin Watts
338 Euston Road, London NW1 3BH

Franklin Watts Australia
Level 17/207 Kent Street
Sydney NSW 2000

Editors: Rachel Tonkin and Julia Bird
Designer: Proof Books
Picture researcher: Diana Morris

Picture credits:
Heather Angel/Natural Visions: 19; Robert Clay/Alamy: 29;
David M Dennis/OSF: front cover, 1, 24; Paul Franklin/OSF: 26;
Raymond Gehman/Alamy: 20; Daniel Heuclin/NHPA: 18; Corey
Hochachka/Design Pics/Corbis: 10; Steven J Kazlowski/Alamy: 7.
Fabio Liverani/Nature PL: 25t; David Manning/Papilio: 11;
Chris Mattison/FLPA/Corbis: 15; Chartchai MeeDang Nin/PD: 16.
David A. Northcott/Corbis: 8; William Osborn/Nature PL: 6; Justine
Pickett/Papilio: 4; Tod Pusser/Nature PL: 9, 21, 25b; Gary Sargent/PD: 5,
23; Kennan Ward/Corbis: 28; Maximillian Weinziergl/Alamy: 12, 13, 17,
27; Doug Weschsler/Nature PL: 2.

Every attempt has been made to clear copyright.
Should there be any inadvertent omission please
apply to the publisher for rectification.

A CIP catalogue record for this book
is available from the British Library

ISBN: 978 0 7496 7062 7

Dewey Classification: 639.3'78

Printed in China

Franklin Watts is a division of Hachette Children's Books,
an Hachette Livre UK company.

Contents

What is a salamander?

Salamanders can live in water and on land. They belong to a group of animals called amphibians, which also includes frogs and toads. Salamanders have long tails, slender bodies and short legs. Although their body shape looks a bit like a lizard's, salamanders are completely different. Their skin is moist, while a lizard's is dry and scaly.

Types of salamander

There are hundreds of different types of salamander. Some are just a few centimetres long, but the biggest can grow to more than 1.5 metres. Most kinds can be kept as pets, but some are easier to look after than others. Newts are a type of salamander. You can tell them from other salamanders because they don't have a groove along the side of their body.

The fire salamander is a handsome and popular pet.

Hatching in water

Most salamanders lay their eggs in water. When they hatch, they are in their larval stage. Like a frog in its tadpole stage, a larval salamander has gills – frilly flaps on the sides of its head that allow it to 'breathe' underwater.

Living on land

Slowly, the larval salamander loses its gills and grows legs. As an adult, it can live on land. The transformation from larva to adult salamander is called metamorphosis. Not all salamanders go through this big change. The red-backed salamander, for example, lays her eggs on land and they hatch into four-legged miniature adults.

Other ways of living

The axolotl is another salamander that does not go through metamorphosis. It remains a larva and lives in water for its whole life. It can breed in its larval form. The Eastern newt is different again. Instead of having the usual two life stages, it has three! In the early autumn, the larva leaves the water, loses its gills and becomes a brightly-coloured, terrestrial creature known as an eft. It lives on land as an eft for up to five years before returning to live in the water once more.

This is a red eft – an Eastern newt in its terrestrial stage. Eventually it will return to the water to live and breed.

Live births

Not all salamanders lay eggs. A few, such as the fire salamander, give birth to live young.

Pet salamanders

Some people collect salamanders from the wild to keep as pets. This is not a good idea because many wild salamanders are endangered (at risk of dying out). In some places, it is even against the law. If you want to keep a pet salamander, go to a specialist breeder and buy an animal that has been bred to live in captivity.

Questions & Answers

✶ **What is an aquatic salamander?**
Salamanders that live in water are called aquatic. Most salamanders live in water for up to two years in the larval stage. Others are aquatic their whole lives.

✶ **What is a terrestrial salamander?**
Terrestrial means living on land. Most adult salamanders live on land. However, they prefer damp places where their skin will not dry out, and they often stay close to ponds and rivers, where they can lay their eggs.

✶ **How long do salamanders live?**
Most salamanders live for five to ten years, but a few can live as long as 25 years. The record-breaker is the Chinese giant salamander, which can live to be 70.

Do you really want a salamander?

Many pets can be stroked and played with. Salamanders are not that kind of pet. They are fascinating to watch, but you should not handle them. The salts and oils on your skin can harm them. Before you go out to buy a salamander, make sure you are ready for the responsibility of feeding it every day and keeping its home clean.

Tiger salamanders are naturally more friendly and responsive that some other kinds of salamanders.

Attention seeking

If you want a friendly pet, salamanders are probably not for you. Most are very shy and stay out of sight a lot of the time. However, some salamanders eventually learn to respond to their owners. They might come to the side of the tank as you approach to feed them.

Toxic pets

Many salamanders and newts produce toxins from their skin to protect themselves from predators. If you touch a salamander – for example, if you are moving it so that you can clean out its tank – make sure you wash your hands thoroughly with soap afterwards.

Time consuming

Salamanders do not need you to play with them, but you will still need to set aside time for them each day. That is because most salamanders are meat-eaters and they like to eat live food. You will need to go to look for worms and other foodstuffs – whatever the weather.

Bad biter

Smaller salamanders may nip, but their bite isn't painful. Watch out for larger species, though, such as the amphiuma.

Questions & Answers

* **Are all salamanders poisonous?**
  No. The ones that produce toxins from their skin are usually brightly coloured. In the wild, this warns predators to stay away.

* **Which are the most dangerous salamanders?**
  Taricha newts produce a powerful toxin called a tarichotoxin. If it is taken in large enough quantities, either by swallowing or through broken skin, it can cause a heart attack in humans.

* **Can I touch a salamander if I have cuts on my hand?**
  No! If you have an open cut, toxins from your pet could enter your blood system. If you have cuts and need to move your pets, ask someone else to help or wear latex gloves.

Costing it out

Salamanders do not cost much to buy or to keep, especially if you collect their food from the wild. However, a tank can be quite expensive to buy. Depending on the species, you may also need a heater or an aquatic pump. Buying a second-hand tank can help to cut the cost.

Being an observer

One of the most rewarding aspects of keeping salamanders is finding out more about their lifecycles and behaviour. You could join a herpetological society (a group interested in reptiles and amphibians) and share your observations and knowledge.

The rough skin newt may look harmless, but its skin releases powerful toxins.

Salamander families

Before choosing your pet salamander, it is a good idea to find out more about the different species of salamanders. You can narrow down your search by looking at the different salamander families. All of the species within a family share certain characteristics.

Same salamanders

Animal groups and families have Latin names to make them identifiable to scientists all over the world. Fire salamanders and all newts belong to the Salamandridae family. Most members of this family live in water as larvae and on land as adults.

Lungless salamanders

There are nearly 250 species of lungless salamander. As their name suggests, they do not have lungs. Instead, they take in oxygen through their moist, slimy skin. Lungless species kept as pets include the dusky salamander, red-backed salamander, northern red salamander and slimy salamander.

Lungless slimy salamanders have a gluey substance on their skin that helps to protect them from predators.

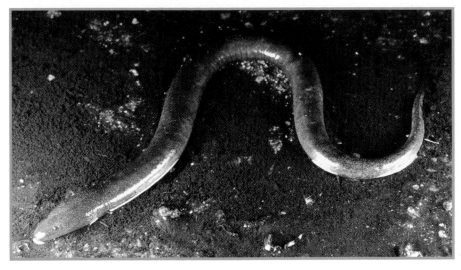

The two-toed amphiuma is shy and nocturnal (active at night).

Water weirdoes

Amphiumas and sirens are both unusual salamanders, rarely kept as pets. Both are aquatic. Amphiumas have tiny, useless legs and only leave the water on very wet nights to seek out new breeding ponds. Sirens look like eels, with no back legs and only tiny front ones.

Mole salamanders

Members of the Ambystomatidae family are nicknamed mole salamanders because they like burrowing. They include the marbled salamander, tiger salamander and spotted salamander, all of which have strong, bold markings. Some kinds of tiger salamander never grow up, and breed in their aquatic form. This family also includes the aquatic axolotl.

Life without light

The olm is one of the oddest salamanders. It can lay eggs or have live young, depending on conditions in the dark cave where it lives.

Mudpuppies

Native to North America, mudpuppies are tricky to keep as pets. In the wild, they are found in a range of habitats including rivers, streams, lakes and swamps. They tend to feed at night, spending the day hiding under stones and logs. They have slimy, long, flattened bodies and very frilly gills.

Questions & Answers

✻ **Which is the easiest terrestrial salamander to keep as a pet?**
Fire salamanders are very popular pets with colourful markings. They need a moist, cool environment, with plenty of hiding places. Mole salamanders make good pets too.

✻ **Which is the easiest aquatic salamander to keep as a pet?**
The Mexican axolotl is hardy and easy to keep. It grows up to 30cm long, so its tank should be at least 60 x 30 x 30cm (length x height x width).

✻ **Which salamanders are most difficult to keep?**
Hellbenders are large, aquatic salamanders. They are so particular about water quality that they are best left to the experts. They also need a lot of space and can give a painful bite.

Buying your salamander

Once you have decided what kind of salamander you want to keep, you need to find a specialist pet shop or a breeder. In the past, many people collected salamanders from the wild. That is no longer acceptable, partly because some salamanders are endangered, but also because it is unfair to make wild animals adapt to a life in captivity.

Where to buy

If you have friends that keep salamanders, they may be able to recommend a good breeder or specialist pet shop. You could also contact your local herpetological society or an animal welfare association (see page 31) for advice.

Choose pets that have clear, glossy skin like these young fire salamanders.

Good conditions

When you visit a breeder, trust your first impressions! The place should be clean and tidy, not dirty and smelly. Check that the tanks do not look overcrowded. There should not be any dead salamanders mixed in with the live ones.

What to look for

Choose a salamander that looks plump and rounded. A sunken belly probably means it has not been fed properly, and this will make it more prone to illness in the future. The salamander's eyes should be bright and its skin should be sleek. Never buy an animal that has sores or traces of fungus on its skin.

Internet shopping

Online pet shops sell specimens from a range of breeders. You won't be able to examine individual specimens before you buy, so see if you can find any testimonials (customer feedback) online. Your new pet should be delivered in a polystyrene box with air holes and a heat pack to keep it warm.

Lots of axolotls

The axolotl is endangered in the wild, but huge numbers are bred in captivity each year.

Where not to buy

Most countries have laws to protect animals that are sold as pets. However, some dealers ignore these laws. They care more about money than animal welfare. If you buy from them, they will carry on keeping their animals in poor conditions – and you will probably get a weak and unhealthy pet.

Questions & Answers

✳ Is it OK to handle my pet before buying?
Salamanders should not be handled too often, but do hold them before you buy so you can have a good look at your pet. Just remember to wash your hands before and after.

✳ Is travelling stressful for salamanders?
Yes. Use a box with a lid and air holes, and pack it loosely with soft, damp peat or sphagnum moss (see page 17). A polystyrene carrying box with air holes will help to keep the temperature constant.

✳ What if I'm transporting aquatic salamanders?
Aquatic salamanders are transported in the same way as aquarium fish. The breeder will use doubled-up plastic bags, half-filled with water and then inflated with air or oxygen.

Hold a salamander very carefully and remember not to handle it for too long, as oils from your hand will harm its delicate skin.

Housing salamanders

A big part of the fun of keeping salamanders is creating a home for them that is as close to nature as possible. Depending on the species, your pets will need a terrarium (a tank with just land, no water), an aqua-terrarium (a tank that is half-water and half-land) or an aquarium (a tank with just water, no land).

This terrarium contains plants and moss. Moss holds water and helps to keep the tank damp.

Choosing your tank

The size of your tank should depend on the size and number of your pets. A fire salamander, for example, grows to around 30cm. A tank for one animal should be at least 90 x 38 x 30cm (length x height x width). If you want to keep two, the tank should be at least 120 x 38 x 30cm. If you are in any doubt, ask the breeder or pet shop supplying your salamander for advice.

Setting up a terrarium

Terrestrial species of salamanders like cool, moist environments. Line the tank with some gravel, then add a thick layer of soil or peat and some damp moss. A shallow dish of water will help to keep the atmosphere humid. Remember not to make your tank too crowded or it will be difficult to clean out.

Lighting

Never put a tank in direct sunlight. Use artificial lighting and turn it on and off to give your pet a proper day and night. You can buy a timer to control this. Ask for advice when buying fluorescent tubes or other bulbs and make sure you buy ones that won't overheat the tank.

Questions & Answers

* **Which salamanders need to live in a terrarium?**
Terrestrial salamanders include fire salamanders, red-backed salamanders, marbled salamanders, tiger salamanders and spotted salamanders. Banded newts also prefer just land.

* **Which salamanders need to live in an aqua-terrarium?**
Most newts enjoy life in an aqua-terrarium. Newts kept as pets include alpine newts, crested newts, eastern newts, emperor newts and marbled newts. The northern red salamander and the Japanese fire-bellied salamander also need a combination of land and water.

* **Which salamanders need to live in an aquarium?**
Hellbenders, sirens, mudpuppies and amphiumas are all aquatic, but only a few specialists keep them in captivity. The axolotl is the only aquatic salamander that is popularly kept as a pet.

Heating

Salamanders from temperate climates will not usually require extra heating, but salamanders from semi-tropical and tropical habitats will. Check your salamander's needs when you buy it. You can heat an aquarium with a water heater, while a terrarium should be warmed with heating pads, placed under the floor covering. Aim to provide a warmer and cooler end of the tank and adjust the temperature to drop slightly at night to mimic the difference between night and day in the salamander's natural habitat.

Escape artists

Your terrarium needs a lid to stop your pet from crawling out. If it escapes, it can dry out and die, or be eaten by another animal. Lids stop the air circulating, though. To stop the tank getting too humid and mouldy, make sure it is ventilated with small air holes and clean it out regularly (see pages 20–21).

Salamanders like to have somewhere to hide away in their tank, so it is important to provide them with rocks, bits of bark and plants.

Specialist housing

Salamanders that live partly on land and partly in water will need to be housed in an aqua-terrarium. You can buy purpose-made aqua-terrariums from most pet shops that specialise in amphibians, or you can try making your own. Set up the land area like an ordinary terrarium, with gravel, soil and moss and join it to the water with rocks or pieces of wood.

About your aqua-terrarium

The water side of an aqua-terrarium is set up and looked after in the same way as an aquarium. Find out what volume of water your species will need. You will need a tank at least 90 x 30 x 30cm (length x height x width) to house a pair of newts, for example.

An aqua-terrarium makes a good home for a marbled newt.

From land to water

Connect the land and water parts of the tank with a piece of rock or wood. Your pet will be able to clamber on to this from the water, and may also use it for basking. Choose wood that is smooth and won't rot, such as ironwood or bogwood.

Removing waste

Salamanders produce a lot of waste. Having a big tank helps to dilute this, but you will also need a good filter. A power filter is fine, but make sure you set it so that the current is not too strong. You can also buy 'friendly' bacteria that break down the harmful ammonia produced by waste accumulating in the tank water.

Gravel

You may want to use gravel in your aquarium to hold the plants in place. Make sure the gravel is not too fine, otherwise your pet may suck it in while feeding. Gravel should be smooth, too, so that your pets do not snag their skin on it.

The great outdoors

Native salamanders can be kept in a garden pond. Enclose it so your specimens do not escape!

Let it stand

When you have just set up an aquarium or aqua-terrarium, do not add animals straight away. Leave it with the filter running for at least 24 hours. You will be able to check that everything is working properly and enable the water to reach room temperature – or warmer, if you're keeping tropical species and using a water heater.

Questions & Answers

❋ **Can I fill my aquarium with water straight from the tap?**
It is best not to because it probably contains chlorine or chloramine – chemicals that kill bacteria. These chemicals make water safe to drink for us, but they can cause sickness or death in salamanders.

❋ **Is there any way of making tap water safe?**
Yes, you can add dechlorinating tablets to it. Buy ones that remove chloramine as well as chlorine. Another way to get rid of the chemicals in tap water is to stand it in an open container for 24 hours.

❋ **Can I put rainwater in my aquarium?**
No, rainwater may be too acidic for your salamanders. You can test for this, but not for the other dangerous chemicals that the rain may contain. It is safest to stick to dechlorinated or bottled (but not distilled) water.

Japanese fire-bellied newts prefer an aquatic set-up, but should also be provided with a small land area of smooth wood or rocks where they can rest.

Plant life

Plants help your salamander to feel at home. You can buy plants for land or for water and they can be real or fake. Think about the advantages and disadvantages of each, then buy what suits you and your pets. As well as making your tank look attractive, plants have some important practical purposes.

Making oxygen

To stay alive, living plants produce their own sugary food. In the process, they take in carbon dioxide from the air or water, and give out oxygen in return. This is very helpful to salamanders, who take in oxygen when they breathe in, and give out carbon dioxide when they breathe out.

Shelter and shade

Plants offer your salamander hiding places. They also provide shade from the tank light, which is usually fitted into the lid. As well as reducing light levels, the layers of leaves can help to keep the temperature cool.

Caring for living plants

All living plants need light to survive, although some types, such as devil's ivy, can cope with relatively low light levels. To keep your plants looking good and to limit their growth, you should clip their leaves and stems regularly. Remember that your plants will need water, too.

Devil's ivy (*Epipremnum aureum*) is readily available and easy to look after.

Aquatic plants help to create a pondlike habitat for this newt.

Questions & Answers

✳ **Which plants are good for terrariums?**
Most houseplants will work fine in a terrarium, but devil's ivy is especially good. It is a kind of vine that you can plant underwater or in damp sphagnum moss. It also puts out roots that take in moisture from the air.

✳ **Which plants are good for aquariums?**
You can use any aquatic plant that is sold for coldwater fish tanks. Eel grass (*Vallisneria gigantean*) and waterweed (*Elodea densa*) are good ones to start with.

✳ **How many plants will I need?**
Ask at the pet shop to see how many plants your tank can take. You will have to replace the plants every now and then.

Fake plants

Artificial plants do not produce oxygen, but they have other advantages. They do not need light or water to survive, and they do not grow old and straggly. You can also cut or bend them to make shelters and hideaways for your pets.

Water carrier
Sphagnum moss can hold up to 20 times its dry weight in water!

Buying artificial plants

Silk plants should only be used in terrariums. Use either real or plastic plants for aquariums, but make sure first that the plastic plants do not contain any wire that could rust and poison the water in your tank.

Food and diet

Most salamanders are meat-eaters that hunt their own food. To supply your pets with food, you may have to turn hunter yourself. Collecting insects and other small invertebrates from the wild is much easier in summer, when bugs are plentiful and there is light for longer. In winter, you may prefer to buy food, or raise your own.

Salamander senses

Terrestrial salamanders hunt by responding to movement, so it is important that some of their food is alive. Aquatic salamanders use other senses, such as smell, to locate a meal. They do need live food, but you can also give them dead insects, fish pellets or even the odd strip of raw beef.

A varied diet

No one foodstuff will meet all of your pet's needs. Try to provide as wide a variety of prey as possible. Use a small jar to collect woodlice, beetles, earthworms and small moths from the wild. Once or twice a week, dust them with powdered vitamin and mineral supplements before feeding them to your salamanders.

Fire salamanders will feed on earthworms and other live foods, such as slugs and crickets.

18

Raising prey

Some prey animals can be raised at home. You can buy young fruit flies, crickets, cockroaches, waxworms, earthworms and whiteworms by mail order or from your local pet shop. Remember to ask how they need to be kept and what food they need. Tropical fish flakes are good for crickets and earthworms.

Household pests

Maggots are a good food for your pets, but make sure they all get eaten – otherwise your house will be plagued by flies when the maggots hatch!

Buying prey

Grasshoppers and locusts are hard to catch or breed, but you may be able to buy them from pet shops. You can also buy hairless baby mice (nicknamed 'pinkies') which are popular with axolotls. Always use shop-bought mice, as wild mice may carry diseases or parasites.

Aquatic foods

Most pet shops or aquariums sell two types of live aquatic food: daphnia (water fleas) and tubifex worms (bloodworms). Never collect aquatic food from the wild. You may introduce pests along with the pond water. Dragonfly larvae, for example, can attack salamanders.

Tubifex worms are readily available from almost any pet shop.

Questions & Answers

✳ **Can I feed mealworms to my salamanders?**
Yes, but ask an adult to help you crush their heads first so they cannot bite and injure your pets. Mealworms are nutritious and are available from most pet shops.

✳ **Can I feed ants to my salamanders?**
It depends. Ants are the main food for wild slimy salamanders. However, ants have powerful jaws and may bite your pets. They also produce a substance called formic acid that is dangerous to some salamanders, so check first.

✳ **Is it possible to give my pets too much food?**
Yes. Just give your pets as much food as they can eat in one go. That way, you will avoid problems such as the prey food multiplying and becoming pests, or of them dying and rotting in the tank.

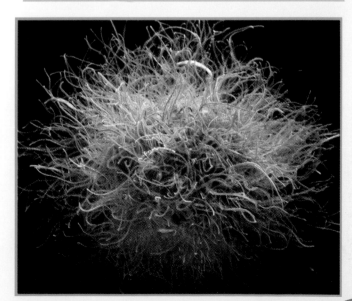

Cleaning the tank

Salamanders thrive in damp, humid conditions, but so do fungi and bacteria. These organisms can affect the health of your pets if they build up too much, while mould on the tank walls can prevent you from being able to view your pets.

Cleaning kit

If you can, keep a bucket that you only use for cleaning out the tank. Make sure it has never had soap, detergent or bleach in it, as all of these can be harmful to your salamander. Hot water and salt are all you need to clean out your tank.

Moving house

It is much easier to clean out the tank when your salamander is not in it. Scoop up aquatic species with a net and put them into a small tank or bucket. Terrestrial salamanders or newts should be placed in a ventilated box lined with damp sphagnum moss.

What to do

Aim to clean out the tank around once a fortnight. First, scrub the tank and its contents with hot, salty water. If decorative rocks, pieces of wood or plastic plants become really dirty, you can soak them overnight. If you have time, allow everything to air dry. Then set up your tank again, using rinsed gravel and fresh peat and sphagnum moss.

Use a small net to gently scoop up aquatic salamanders from their tank.

Cleaning an aquarium

With an aquarium, you need to avoid a build-up of ammonia (see page 14) from your pets' urine. A complete water change is too stressful for your salamanders. Instead, use a siphon to remove about a third of the water, and poke it into the gravel to suck away any dirt at the same time. Top up the tank with dechlorinated, room-temperature water.

Up the wall

Salamanders can walk up glass walls. Sticky mucus produced from pads on their feet gives them grip.

Questions & Answers

✳ **Can I use bleach to clean my tank?**
It is safer to stick to hot water. Using weak bleach can be fine if the tank is thoroughly rinsed, but it is very hard to be sure that no traces of bleach remain.

✳ **Should I clean my aquarium filter with hot water?**
No. Clean everything else with hot water, but not your filter. Use cool water that won't kill its friendly bacteria.

✳ **What will happen if I don't clean out my aquarium regularly?**
Aquatic salamanders slowly adapt to poor water. When you finally do clean the tank, the shock may kill your pet. Another problem with dirty tanks is that you will not be able to introduce any new animals.

The big clean

Every six weeks or so, give your aquarium a more thorough clean. Siphon off the water into a bucket. Halfway through, transfer your pets into it with a net. Scrub out the tank and clean the gravel and any rocks in hot water. Use old water to refill two-thirds of the tank, then top it up with clean, dechlorinated water as usual.

Salamanders take in oxygen and moisture through their skin, so it is very important to prevent poisons building up in the tank.

Salamander companions

Salamanders are quite happy living alone. However, you may decide that you want to keep more than one so that your tank is more interesting to watch. Another reason might be if you want to breed salamanders (see pages 24–25). Check before keeping salamanders of different species together – some kinds do not get on.

Mixed species

Ask advice from an expert before you try to put salamanders from different species together in the same tank. Salamanders release toxins from their skin, especially when they feel stressed or threatened. These toxins could prove fatal to other species.

Parasite crossover

Another reason for not mixing salamander species is that each salamander carries particular parasites. These are organisms that live inside it, usually without causing harm. Problems can arise if parasites move from one species of salamander to another. With no resistance to a new parasite, a salamander can grow ill and even die.

The spotted salamander can be housed with other types of salamanders from a similar environment.

Shared habitats

If you want to keep mixed species together, it makes sense to choose animals that come from similar habitats in the wild. You could set up a terrarium for slimy salamanders, marbled salamanders and spotted salamanders to share, for example. All three are native to the moist woodlands of the eastern United States.

Different habitats

Another possibility for a mixed tank is to choose two species that are native to the same area, but whose paths rarely cross because one is terrestrial and one is aquatic. In this sort of set-up, it helps if the species grow to a similar size. Red-backed salamanders and eastern newts can be kept in the same aqua-terrarium, for example.

Top team

Mating pairs of red-backed salamanders work together to defend their territory and to protect their eggs and hatchlings.

Fighting

Some terrestrial salamanders are used to having a home range that they defend. They mark the edges of their range with mucus or faeces, and fight rivals that try to enter the area. Red-backed salamanders are one of the most territorial species and can be aggressive towards one another.

Questions & Answers

✳ **Do salamanders ever bite each other's legs off?**
If one of your pets is lacking a limb or a tail, it is far more likely that it dropped off. Salamanders do this deliberately to distract predators while they make a getaway.

✳ **Can legs and tails regrow?**
Yes! Salamanders and newts are famous for being able to do this. It is called regeneration. Depending on the animal's age and size, it takes between four and 12 weeks to grow a new leg or tail. The new limb grows blood vessels, muscles and nerves, and is properly connected to the rest of the body.

Red-backed salamanders can live together, as long as the tank is large enough for each to have its own hiding places.

Breeding salamanders

Breeding salamanders is complicated but very rewarding. You should only try it if you have lots of experience in looking after salamanders and have support from an adult. Breeding habits vary from species to species, but most salamanders reproduce at a particular time of year. You will need to change the conditions in the tank so that your pets think the seasons are changing.

A mating pair of Jordan's salamanders from the eastern United States.

The salamander's year

In the wild, most salamanders breed in the spring after their winter sleep. One way to make your pets breed is to encourage them to hibernate. Slowly reduce the temperature in the tank so that your pets think that it is winter. Ask an expert for advice before you do this.

Light levels

To convince your salamanders that the seasons really are changing, you will need change the hours of daylight, too. As you drop the temperature, reduce the hours of daylight to mimic winter. As you raise the temperature again, increase the hours of daylight to mimic spring.

Dressing up

It is hard to tell the difference between male and female salamanders except during the breeding season. Keeping lots of animals is one way to be sure that you will get a breeding pair, but it is not really practical. Some salamanders become very showy around mating time. The male banded newt develops a crest that is twice the depth of its body. This colourful salamander has a brown spotted body, orange belly and stripes down its sides. It also has blue and green mottled crests on each side of its tail.

The colourful markings of the great crested newt help it to attract a mate.

Captive breeders

Wild axolotls only live and breed in two lakes in Mexico. Pet ones are bred all over the world!

Baby care

If you are lucky enough for your pets to breed and their eggs to hatch, be prepared! Find out what the larvae will need. Axolotl babies require lots of space, otherwise they may eat each other. Brine shrimp and chopped blackworms are good foodstuffs for most larvae.

These tiger salamander eggs are protected by a big mass of jelly.

Questions & Answers

✳ **Do all salamanders lay eggs?**
Most do, usually in water but sometimes on land. Laying can happen straight after fertilisation or weeks later, depending on the species. The number of eggs also vary. The Spanish ribbed newt can lay as many as a thousand eggs at a time.

✳ **Do any salamanders guard their eggs?**
Many abandon their eggs, but some take care of them until they hatch. A female amphiuma stays coiled around her eggs for five months.

✳ **Do any salamanders have live young?**
Yes. The red-backed salamander has young that hatch out as perfectly formed miniature adults.

Sick salamanders

One of the trickiest things about keeping salamanders is spotting when they are ill. With experience, though, you will be able to detect illness through a range of clues. If you pick up on these early enough, you can nurse your pets back to health by adjusting their environment or diet, or by treating them with medicine.

Secret signs

Watching your pets when they are healthy will help you to notice unusual behaviour. Has your salamander moved from its usual place in the tank? Perhaps it is being bullied by a tank mate. Is it moving in a strange way? A pulsing throat might be a sign of heat stress.

Sores and wounds

Salamanders have very thin, sensitive skin that is easily damaged. Open wounds can become infected by bacteria. Symptoms include refusing food, losing weight or slime building up on the skin. The only treatment is antibiotics, so you will need to get advice from a vet.

Skin diseases

Like aquarium fish, aquatic salamanders often catch fungal infections. The best way to avoid these is to house new pets on their own for at least 21 days before introducing them to your tank. Fungal skin infections can be fatal if they are not caught early on. They are treated with drops added to the tank water. Ask your pet shop or vet for advice.

Aquatic salamanders can suffer from fungal diseases. Watch out for unusual colouring, inflammation or sores on the skin.

Salmonella

Salmonella is a bacterial infection that makes salamanders' organs swell up and eventually causes death. The treatment only works for aquatic species and takes nearly three weeks. It involves adding an antibiotic called terramycin and salt to the water.

Axolotls can develop salmonella, but they can be treated for it.

Fire survivor

People used to say that salamanders could survive fire, perhaps because they have a moist skin to protect them. This is not true, however!

Finding a vet

Many vets have relatively limited experience of treating amphibians. However, it is still worth getting in touch with your vet if your salamander is ill. He or she will have access to experts and should be able to help you.

Questions & Answers

✱ **What should I do if one of my salamanders looks ill?**
Move it to a separate tank straight away, so it cannot infect your other pets.

✱ **What should I do if one of my salamanders dies?**
It is sad when any pet dies. You might find it helps to bury it and mark its grave in some way. Take photos of all your pets when they are alive, so that you have something to remember them by.

✱ **How can I find out what my pet died of?**
If you are not sure why your pet died, consider sending it to the vet for an autopsy. This is expensive, but can be helpful if you are worried about its tankmates.

27

Endangered salamanders

Salamanders are becoming increasingly endangered in the wild. Today, some pet keepers are helping to protect salamander populations, and are even returning animals to the wild. Once you have grown to love amphibians, you will want to do all you can to look after them, in your home or in their natural habitat.

Under threat

There are many different reasons why salamanders are at risk. Some salamanders have lost their natural habitats. Over the last 50 years, many ancient woodlands and marshes have been cleared so that new homes, roads and factories can be built.

Many salamanders, such as this California newt, are now very rare in the wild.

Pollution

Another problem is that salamanders are extremely sensitive to changes in their environment because they 'breathe' through their skin. They often take in pollutants, such as dangerous chemicals from car exhaust fumes, factory chimneys and other places, from the air or in water.

Giving your time

Some conservation groups use volunteers to help salamanders cross the road during the breeding season, when salamanders head back to their breeding ponds in huge numbers. Helping out can save thousands of salamander lives. Clearing rubbish from local streams and ponds can be another way to help.

Zoos and wildlife parks

One way to get close to some really interesting salamanders is to be a volunteer at your local zoo or conservation centre. You can help educate other people about these amazing animals and you will gain lots of practical experience at the same time.

Questions & Answers

✳ **Why are salamanders at extra risk in the breeding season?**

Many travel long distances to find a place to breed. They use sight and smell to return to the pond where they grew up. Along the way, many are picked off by predators or run over by cars.

✳ **Why do we need to count salamanders?**

Salamanders spend much of the time hiding or hibernating. Unless volunteers help out with surveys and field counts, experts will not be able to see how endangered wild salamanders really are.

✳ **Could acid rain or climate change be affecting salamanders?**

Perhaps. One very simple way that you can help salamanders living in the wild is to try to be as environmentally friendly as you can.

This sign warns motorists and other road users to slow down. Newts cross this road to reach their breeding spots.

Salamander subway

In some areas of the United States, tunnels have been built so that salamanders can pass safely under busy roads.

29

Glossary

ammonia
A smelly substance found in urine. When it builds up in an aquarium, it can make the water poisonous.

amphibian
A cold-blooded animal that has a bony skeleton and slimy skin. Amphibians are adapted to live partly on land and partly in water.

aqua-terrarium
A tank that is half-aquarium and half-terrarium.

aquatic
Living in water.

autopsy
An examination of a dead body to find out the reason(s) for the death.

bacteria
Microscopic living things, many of which can cause disease.

captivity
Kept in a contained space, rather than free to roam in the wild.

carbon dioxide
A gas produced by animals when they breathe out.

characteristics
Features or qualities that animals have in common.

chlorine
A chemical that is added to tap water to kill germs (chloramine is another). Both are harmful to salamanders.

diet
The food that animals usually eat. Salamanders should have a healthy, varied diet.

endangered
In danger of extinction.

faeces
Droppings.

fertilisation
Adding the male sex cell (sperm) to the female sex cell (egg) to make a new life.

filter
A machine that takes in aquarium water, sieves out particles of dirt and then returns the cleaned water to the tank.

gills
Feathery body parts used for taking in oxygen from water.

habitat
The place where an animal lives in the wild.

herpetology
The study of reptiles and amphibians.

hibernate
To hide away or sleep during the cold part of the year.

home range
The area in which an animal usually moves around to find shelter, food and a mate.

humid
Damp.

invertebrates
Animals without backbones, including insects, spiders and shellfish.

larva (plural larvae)
The name for the young of certain animals, including salamanders and many insects.

metamorphosis
A complete change in the appearance of an animal, for example from a tadpole into a frog, as part of its lifecycle.

oxygen
A gas found in air and water that all animals need to breathe in order to stay alive.

predator
An animal that hunts other animals.

reproduce
To have babies or breed.

siphon
A plastic tube used to suck up water from the tank.

species
A group of one type of animal or plant.

temperate
A mild climate, neither hot nor cold.

terrarium
A tank for land animals.

terrestrial
Living on land.

toxin
A poison.

tropical
From the hot, humid climate of the tropics.

Further information

If you want to learn more about salamanders, buying salamanders, looking after salamanders, or if you would like to get involved in animal welfare, here are some helpful websites:

UNITED KINGDOM
The British Herpetological Society
A society that studies and protects British amphibians and reptiles.
Website: www.thebhs.org
Contact address:
11 Strathmore Place
Montrose
Angus DD10 8LQ

The Herpetological Conservation Trust
A charity set up to protect amphibians and reptiles. Its website includes details on all native British amphibians.
Website: www.herpconstrust.org.uk
Contact address:
655a Christchurch Road
Boscombe
Bournemouth
Dorset BH1 4AP

The Reptile Experience
This husband-and-wife team specialise in keeping reptiles, but their website includes notes on caring for many unusual pets, including salamanders and newts.
Website: www.reptilehouse.net

Royal Society for the Prevention of Cruelty to Animals (RSPCA)
Campaigning charity for all animals.
The website includes newsletters and animal care advice.
Website: www.rspca.org.uk
Contact address:
Enquiries service
RSPCA
Wilberforce Way,
Southwater
Horsham, West Sussex RH13 9RS
Tel: 0870 333 5999

AUSTRALIA
The Australian Herpetological Society
A national society for people interested in keeping reptiles and amphibians as pets.
Website: www.ahs.org.au

INTERNATIONAL
Scales and Tails
An outreach organisation that educates and entertains.
Website: www.scalesandtails.com

Amphibian Species of the World
An online reference hosted by the American Museum of Natural History that lists all amphibian species of the world.
See: http://research.amnh.org/herpetology/amphibia/index.php

Amphibiaweb
A free online resource for finding out about amphibian biology and conservation.
Website: www.amphibiaweb.org

Global Amphibian Assessment
A project dedicated to assessing the extinction and conservation of Red List (endangered) amphibian species, including salamanders and newts.
Website: www.globalamphibians.org

Note to parents and teachers: Every effort has been made by the Publishers to ensure that these websites are suitable for children, that they are of the highest educational value, and that they contain no inappropriate or offensive material. However, because of the nature of the Internet, it is impossible to guarantee that the contents of these sites will not be altered. We strongly advise that Internet access is supervised by a responsible adult.

Index